ENGLISH PORCELAIN

John Cushion

Former Senior Research Assistant
Department of Ceramics
Victoria and Albert Museum, London

Charles Letts Books Limited

The author would like to express his gratitude to the acknowledged collectors and dealers, for their kindness and willing co-operation in making the pieces illustrated in this volume available for study and photography. Some of the pieces illustrated may, by now, have changed ownership.

Especial thanks are also due to Mr. George Savage, the well-known authority of a wide range of antiques, for his help in many ways.

First published 1974
Revised edition 1982
by Charles Letts Books Limited
77 Borough Road, London SE1 1DW

Photographs: Michael Dyer Associates

ISBN 0 85097 349 X

Printed and bound by Charles Letts (Scotland) Ltd

CONTENTS

INTRODUCTION 7

INTRODUCTION

The secret of making true or hard-paste porcelain had been known for about nine hundred years before even an artificial porcelain, or soft-paste, was first made in England. The manufacture of true porcelain, as eventually produced by William Cookworthy in 1768, at Plymouth, depended upon knowledge of two basic ingredients, china-clay and china-stone, and the technical ability to build the type of kilns in which the temperature could be controlled up to about 1300°C.

The Chinese potters, who were without doubt the most inventive and skilful potters in the civilized world, had known of the material of china-clay as early as the Han dynasty (206 BC–AD 220). They knew this material as kaolin, meaning 'high-ridge', obviously relating to the region in which it was found. China-clay was used initially in the production of a high-fired stoneware. It was most probably in about AD 850, during the T'ang dynasty (AD 618–906), that the second essential material was located. This was china-stone, or petuntse, meaning 'little white bricks', which was the form in which the pulverised and purified feldspathic stone was prepared for use by the potter. These two materials, when blended together, were fired in wood-burning kilns to a temperature of about 1300°C. The Chinese rather aptly referred to these ingredients as the flesh and skeleton of porcelain, the minute particles of white china-clay serving as a framework for the translucent 'flesh' of china-stone. The transparent glaze, which consisted almost entirely of the china-stone, could be fired together with the body of the ware. The secret of the making of this material was not learnt in Europe until early in the eighteenth century, when the letters of a Jesuit missionary, Père d'Entrecolles, gave full details of the manufacture. He learnt this whilst living in the city of Ching-tê Chên, in the Kiangsi province, the centre of the Chinese ceramic industry. The first Europeans to become conversant with Chinese porcelain, however, were almost certainly the Italians. Marco Polo, when returning from his Far Eastern travels at the end of the thirteenth century, is known to have brought back some examples with him. It is, therefore, not surprising that it was the Italian potters who had initial success in making imitation porcelain; a glassy hybrid material, now referred to as Medici porcelain, which to our knowledge was the first European soft-paste.

Medici porcelain cannot be considered as a commercial ware, it was more the result of a private venture of the Grand Duke Francesco I d'Medici, who sponsored the limited manufacture from about 1575 until his death in 1587. China-clay and china-stone were unknown to the Italian potters, who were engaged primarily in the production of tin-glazed earthenware (*maiolica*). Their soft-paste porcelain consisted of about 80% white-firing clays, together with 20% frit (the ingredients of glass). When fired to about 11000°C it looked similar to true porcelain, but was of a much softer body and far less stable in the kiln. Prior to adding the glaze, which was fired at a second kiln-firing, these wares were decorated with the same underglaze-blue as used by the Chinese potters from about AD 1300. In addition their designs were sometimes outlined with purple, derived from the metallic oxide of manganese.

Continental Porcelain after the 17th Century

To our knowledge no further attempts were made to produce porcelain in Europe until the second half of the seventeenth century, when a glassy soft-paste porcelain was again produced, this time in France, first at Rouen and later at Saint Cloud, near Paris. Details concerning Rouen porcelain are very vague, and wares produced there were apparently few and very difficult to distinguish from those made later in the seventeenth century at Saint Cloud. Here the family of Pierre Chicaneau produced some very fine table-ware and figures, until closing in 1766. Two later factories achieved equal fame. One, patronised by Louis-Henri de Bourbon, Prince de Condé, was established at Chantilly in 1725, the other, patronised by Louis-François de Neufville, Duc de Villeroy, at Mennecy in 1734. Experiments also started at Vincennes as early as 1738, but it was nearer 1750 before the really white and beautiful soft-paste porcelain was produced in any quantity. This production was moved to a newly erected factory at Sèvres, between Vincennes and Paris, in 1756.

For many years large sums of money had been spent by the German Courts on the importation of hard-paste porcelain from the Far East, mostly Chinese and, to a lesser extent, Japanese. During the late years of the seventeenth century, Augustus Rex, Elector of Saxony, King of Poland, had commissioned research into the mineral wealth of the country of Saxony. There were two primary aims, firstly to discover the materials essential for the production of fine glass, and secondly how to manufacture porcelain of the Chinese type and by 1710 a hard-paste porcelain was being made at the Royal Saxon Porcelain Manufactory at Meissen, near Dresden. The Meissen factory must not be confused with the many minor factories and decorating workshops, which sprang up in the city of Dresden itself during the second half of the nineteenth century, in many cases where they merely added enamel colours and gilding in the most popular of Meissen styles, to porcelain made elsewhere in Germany. Many of these small concerns deliberately adopted marks sufficiently similar to the famous crossed-swords of Meissen to confuse the inexperienced purchaser.

Soft-paste Porcelain in England

The English porcelain factories only rarely made entirely original wares. Although there is evidence to suggest that factories did exist at Greenwich, Limehouse and Vauxhall about the middle of the eighteenth century, they must have been in production for a comparatively short period, and their wares have not as yet been identified with certainty. There seems to be little doubt that it was at the London factory in Chelsea, that two Flemish silversmiths, Nicholas Sprimont and Charles Gouyn, first produced a soft-paste porcelain in commercial quantities in this country. Chelsea wares are referred to by collectors as being of a period when a certain type of factory-mark was in use, but such marks were by no means consistently used. From 1745–49 we refer to as the 'incised triangle' period because it was during this time that Chelsea wares were often marked with a small triangle which had been incised, or scratched, into the clay whilst it was still 'green' or 'cheese-hard'.

The mark most commonly used from about 1749–52 is referred to as the 'raised anchor', and consists of a small anchor, raised in relief on an oval medallion, which was then applied to the body of the article before firing. Chemical analysis has recently been used to reveal that during this period, and the following 'red-anchor' period (1752–58), Chelsea usually added a small quantity of tin oxide to their glaze. This was to make it slightly whiter but not entirely opaque, which was sometimes what happened with such Continental factories as Chantilly and Doccia. During Chelsea's final years as an independent factory, the usual mark was an anchor painted in gilt. This 'gold-anchor' period continues from about 1758 until 1770, when the Chelsea factory was taken over by William Duesbury, the proprietor of the Derby porcelain factory. These years, when both factories were run as one concern, are referred to as the 'Chelsea-Derby' period (1770–84).

It has now been proved that from about 1749 until 1754 there were two entirely independent porcelain factories in operation in Chelsea. The second factory is known as the 'Girl-in-a-Swing' factory, a name which refers to an early key figure, used to help identify a whole group of wares now considered to have been made at the same factory. This group is constantly growing now that the style of modelling and the manner and palette of the enamel decoration can be more easily recognised. The 'Girl-in-a-Swing' group were produced from a glassy soft-paste porcelain which contained about double the quantity of lead that was used by Sprimont at his original Chelsea concern.

Recent excavations made in North Staffordshire indicate that a form of porcelain was being produced at the Pomona factory, Newcastle, by William Steers as early as 1744, continuing under Joseph Wilson until 1754. 1749 had also seen a further porcelain factory established by William Jenkinson at Longton Hall, near Newcastle-under-Lyme. The porcelain of Longton Hall was of a very similar body to that of Chelsea's 'Girl-in-a-Swing' factory and rather suggests that it was a Staffordshire potter who had previously been employed at one of the London factories who took the knowledge of soft-paste porcelain manufacture back to The Potteries.

The earliest table-wares and figures made at this factory suggest that the Staffordshire potters were experiencing great difficulty in adapting their skills to the more refined material of porcelain. The factory was never a financial success and closed in 1760.

Chelsea porcelain was expensive, and many of the factory's table-wares were too lavishly decorated to be considered as practical, whereas the other major London factory, Bow, sought to produce good practical table-wares for the mass market. It made large quantities of cheaply produced wares decorated, according to the popular taste of that time, in Chinese style using underglaze-blue, which only necessitated the wares being twice fired for completion.

Thomas Frye and Edward Heylyn's first patent of 1744 concerned with the production of porcelain at Bow, only dealt with the making of the materials essential to the production of porcelain and not the wares themselves. Full-scale production of saleable wares did not take place until nearer 1746–47. Frye and Heylyn were partly financed by a wealthy Cheapside draper, whose obituary notice in 1751 described him as 'George Arnold, Esq., Alderman of Cheap Ward, President of St. Thomas's Hospital and one of the principal proprietors of the Porcelain Manufactory at Bow'. Local rate accounts for 1749 also show the Bow factory as 'Arnold & Comp.'.

There is very little known of the earliest of Bow wares. The first dated examples do not appear before 1750. We are told by Thomas Craft (a factory decorator who wrote in 1790) that 'the Model of the Building was taken from that of Canton in China'; accepting this to be so we can more readily understand why the factory was known as 'New Canton'. This name was also written on some of their early dated examples as 'MADE AT NEW CANTON'.

Bow wares became so popular that at the peak of their production, between 1760–65, there were about 300 hands employed at the factory. The wares were well summed up in the 1761 revised edition of Defoe's *Tour of Great Britain*, where Samuel Richard adds to the original entry, that 'Though not so fine as some made at *Chelsea*, or as that from *Dresden*, it is much stronger than either and therefore better for common Use; and, being much cheaper than any other China, there is a greater demand for it.' The factory closed in 1776.

One now only rarely hears the completely erroneous term 'Chinese Lowestoft' and there is no reason for suggesting that the small factory of Lowestoft in East Anglia ever produced a hard-paste porcelain of the type manufactured in China. The factory was first established in 1760 by four partners, who produced a bone-porcelain very similar in many ways to that made at Bow. Up until about 1768 all their wares were decorated in underglaze-blue, after which enamel colours were also used, until the factory finally closed in about 1801.

Among the most sought-after Lowestoft porcelain are moulded table-wares, such as tea-caddies and jugs, attributed to a factory modeller, James Hughes. A certain class of decoration combining underglaze-blue and enamel colours in a pleasing, yet naïve manner, is referred to by the name of Redgrave, from a family known to have worked at the factory. Lowestoft blue and white porcelain can often be identified by a small blue number painted onto the inside wall of the foot-rims. These are painters' marks, used to identify their work for accounting purposes; the highest recorded number being 17.

Although a limited number of interesting soft-paste porcelain figures were made at Derby from about 1750, it was 1756 before the Derby porcelain factory was established by William Duesbury, who had previously been engaged as a decorator of pottery and porcelain made at many different English factories. Duesbury's earliest wares were mostly in the styles popularised by the German factory of Meissen, but from about 1760 he appears to have turned his attention to the current fashions of the Chelsea factory. His figures made in the Chelsea 'gold-anchor' style can usually be identified by three or more small dark patches on the base. These were the result of supporting the figures on pads of clay during the glaze-firing, a precaution against the glaze 'running' and fusing the piece to the inside of the saggar. In 1770 Duesbury took over the Chelsea concern, and from 1770–84 the wares produced by the two factories are described as being of 'Chelsea-Derby'. Many of the table-wares made during this period were in the current neo-Classical style, and number amongst the finest, and most practical English porcelain examples of the eighteenth century.

In 1749 Benjamin Lund and William Miller established a factory at Bristol. They produced a type of porcelain which had most of the advantages of hard-paste, due to the use of soapstone (steatite), a natural mixture of china-clay and magnesium silicate. This material was quarried under licence in the area of the Lizard, in the West of England. The business continued until 1752, when it was taken over by the Worcester Porcelain Company. There seems little doubt that the Worcester partnership was formed in 1751 with the take-over in view, and the claim of Dr. Wall, one of the foremost partners, that the Worcester factory were the originators of this new type of porcelain, was not strictly true. Worcester is the only English porcelain factory that has continued from its early start to the present day.

The majority of Worcester's eighteenth-century wares showed a great deal of originality by comparison with Chelsea, Bow or Derby as they were not so influenced by Far Eastern or Continental styles of decoration, other than *chinoiserie*. From the time that the factory was purchased by Thomas Flight in 1783, however, their wares became often decidedly dull and were generally inferior to those produced from after about 1790 by Robert Chamberlain and his family. This factory was eventually amalgamated with the Flight, Barr & Barr concern in 1840, continuing until 1852, when the factory came under the proprietorship of Kerr & Binns. In 1862 the Royal Worcester Porcelain Company was formed.

As there were at least eight major concerns manufacturing porcelain in Liverpool during the second half of the eighteenth century, it has in the past been difficult to suggest a definite factory for many examples. Recent research and the excavation of early sites have made this task easier. It is now known, for example, that, contrary to general belief, porcelain figures *were* made at Liverpool. Fragments found on the site of Samuel Gilbody's factory at Shaw's Brow have been used to identify a figure which would almost certainly previously have been attributed to the early Derby period (1756–60).

Credit is given to Josiah Spode (*b.*1733, *d.*1797) for the introduction of the material we know today, bone-china. This body consists basically of approximately 50% calcined animal bone, as used initially at the Bow factory, and the ingredients of true porcelain (25% china-clay, and 25% china-stone) a type of ware in which English potters have specialised. Most other foreign porcelain-producing countries having concentrated on the production of hard-paste wares.

Early factory-marks are best used as confirmation rather than as a rigid guide to attribution, for the more important these early wares are to collectors the more likely one is to encounter fraudulently marked pieces, the marks in some cases having been applied to later reproductions made originally as honest, but late pieces.

Marks which have been impressed or incised into the clay whilst it is still in its plastic condition, are acceptable as having been applied at the time of manufacture, providing they were applied under the glaze. Later grinding into a previously fired body was sometimes used to imitate this type of mark, a practice sometimes seen on biscuit porcelain figures. Marks applied in underglaze-blue must also be of the same period as the piece, but underglaze-greens, reds, pinks and black were only used from the early years of the nineteenth century, chrome being one material used to produce some of these colours.

Enamel or gilt marks are especially dangerous as they can always be added at a later date. These added marks are often seen on the base, accompanied by a small unglazed patch. This usually indicates that a later mark has been ground, or etched, away, to make the added early mark acceptable. Gilding is also used to conceal late marks. Often an exciting Continental porcelain mark may be seen to be accompanied by a small gilt design or flower. This gilding can easily be removed with wire-wool, usually revealing such words as 'Made in France'. Collectors seeking early wares should always avoid any wares marked with the country of origin. It was not until 1890 that the Americans introduced their McKinley Tariff Act, after which time no wares were permitted to be imported into the U.S.A. unless marked with the name of the manufacturing country. Thus the term 'Made in England', etc., usually indicates a date well into this century.

From 1842 English manufacturers patented their designs, or shapes. These pieces usually bear a diamond-shaped mark, with numbers, or letters, in each corner. Ceramic mark-books (see Bibliography) can then be used to decipher this mark, and discover the exact date that the design was registered with the Patent Office. This date is, of course, not necessarily the date that the piece was actually made. From 1884 the 'diamond mark' was replaced simply by a registered number.

Plate I

Pair of salts in the form of shells;
soft-paste porcelain painted in
enamel colours
Mark: an incised triangle
CHELSEA; 1745–49
Diameter 2¾ ins.

John Warrell Collection

There seems little doubt that the soft-paste porcelain factory established at
Chelsea, in London, by 1745, was the first English concern to produce
wares in a commercial quantity. Nicholas Sprimont, the proprietor, was a
Huguenot who had first registered his mark as a silversmith in London in
1742. His work was much admired by Frederick, Prince of Wales, and
several examples of Sprimont's silver are now in the Royal Collection. In
some cases these pieces show a distinct similarity in style to his early
porcelain, which consisted primarily of small table-wares.

   These two salts are typical of the porcelain first produced at Chelsea in
the so-called 'triangle period' of the factory (1745–c.1749), when a mark in
the form of a small triangle was often incised into the clay prior to the
'biscuit' firing. Such marks, when covered by glaze, are always acceptable
as having been applied at the time of manufacture.

   The Chelsea porcelain of this period was of a beautiful soft-paste, which
was apparently a difficult material to handle. Fire cracks, due to irregular
shrinkage, often occurred and any attempt at fine modelling was
invariably obscured by a thick glaze.

   Due to the patronage of Sir Everard Fawkener the Chelsea modellers
and decorators were given access to the very fine collection of Meissen
porcelain of Sir Charles Hanbury Williams, the British Ambassador at the
Court of Dresden. Their early attempts to imitate the fine enamel painting
of this long-established Saxon factory were very poor by comparison, but
showed, nevertheless, a naïve charm which the sophisticated, hard-paste
Continental porcelain lacked.

Plate 2

Dish of silver form; soft-paste
porcelain, painted with enamel
colours
Mark: anchor in relief on applied
oval medallion
CHELSEA; *c.*1749–52
Length 9½ ins.

The dates suggested for the periods of the Chelsea factory must not be
accepted too rigidly. There is no reason to think that the changes in
marking and the variations in the composition of materials took place
simultaneously. Sprimont was constantly experimenting to produce a finer
and more practical material and recent research has proved that from about
1749 a small amount of tin oxide was added to the Chelsea glaze. This was
to help give a whiter appearance to their wares, and it was at about this
same time that a new form of factory-mark was introduced to replace the
incised triangle. This new mark was in the form of a small oval medallion
with a raised anchor in the centre and was again applied prior to the initial
firing and, in consequence, was covered with glaze. The anchor in this
form of mark was frequently picked out with red enamel.

The form of dish illustrated shows, probably better than any other, the
close relationship between Sprimont's silver and his porcelain.

Plate 3

Cup and saucer; soft-paste
porcelain, painted in enamel
colours
Mark: anchor in relief on applied
medallion
CHELSEA; *c*.1750–52
Diameter (of saucer) 5¼ ins.

John Warrell Collection

This cup and saucer illustrates one of the most attractive styles of Chelsea
decoration, which today is also one of the most sought after. Very little is
known concerning the names of the Chelsea decorators, but such fine
work as shown is usually attributed to the 'Fable Painter'. Many ceramic
specialists have carried out research into this particular style of painting and
agree that the man most likely to have been responsible during the later
'red-anchor' period (1752–*c*.1758) is Jeffrey Hamet O'Neale (*d*.1801), a
miniature-painter. Similar decoration, sometimes bearing O'Neale's
signature, can at times be seen on porcelain made later at Worcester, where
O'Neale is known to have lived from about 1768–70.

Such a style of decoration appears on the porcelain of both the 'raised'
and 'red-anchor' periods (1749–52 and 1752–*c*.1758), but the painting on
the cup and saucer illustrated is more likely to be the work of the earlier
decorator, thought by some researchers to be William Duvivier, who died
at Chelsea in 1755. There are certainly some noticeable differences in the
style of the earlier and later painting, the later usually being a little more
accomplished. Present-day collectors of Chelsea porcelain are unanimous
in accepting the so-called 'red-anchor' period of the factory as the peak of
their production as far as quality is concerned. The mark on many wares
and figures made from about 1752 until near 1758 consisted of a small red-
enamel anchor.

Plate 4

Bonbonnière and patch box; soft-paste porcelain, painted in enamel colours, with gilt mounts
CHELSEA; *c.*1755
Heights 3 ins. & 2½ ins.

It was obviously the aim of Sprimont to produce porcelain which would compete in popularity with that of Meissen. His table-wares were in many instances equally attractive, but, due to the nature of the soft-paste porcelain used, were far less practical.

In addition to useful wares Sprimont produced many original objects referred to as 'Chelsea-toys'. These usually took the form of little, costly luxuries such as *bonbonnières*, patch boxes, scent bottles, needle-cases, thimbles, seals, etc. These small objects could be produced more successfully by the English 'slip-casting' method of moulding than by the 'press-moulding' technique, used at Meissen. These toys were especially popular on the Continent and were exported in large quantities, sometimes bearing amorous French inscriptions, which were often mis-spelt.

Similar examples which were, for many years, considered to have been made by Sprimont, are now known to have been produced by a rival factory also operating at Chelsea between about 1749 and 1754. These are inferior in modelling, of a more glassy paste, and can be distinguished by their very distinctive palette, which included strong yellow, crimson, chocolate-colour hair and doll-like eyes. This undertaking is known in the collecting world as the 'Girl-in-a-Swing' factory, so-named after a documentary model, which can be seen in the Victoria and Albert Museum and The Museum of Fine Arts, Boston, Massachusetts.

Plate 5

Figure of a cooper; soft-paste
porcelain, painted in enamel
colours
Mark: an anchor in red enamel
CHELSEA; c.1758
Height 5¼ ins.

John Warrell Collection

This figure of a cooper, with iron rings slung around his shoulder, is a very
rare model and does not seem to appear in any of the major recorded
collections or exhibitions of Chelsea porcelain. The Chelsea porcelain
figures of the 'red-anchor' period are certainly the finest English porcelain
figures ever produced, the majority being inspired by the earlier Meissen
models, most of which were the work of the famous modeller
J. J. Kaendler, or his assistants. The enamels were applied more sparingly at
Chelsea, and because of the softer glaze, these colours tended to be softened
by their fusing into the glaze rather than remaining upon the surface, as is
the case with hard-paste porcelain.

Bases are always a good guide to period, the earlier wares usually having
simple mounds often sprinkled with applied relief flowers. With the
introduction of the rococo style in all the decorative arts of the period,
wave-like scroll-work became fashionable and this, unfortunately,
produced a less animated appearance in many of these figures. The gilt
scroll-work on the base of the cooper suggests a date nearer 1758, when
Chelsea started to mark many of their wares with a gilt anchor.

Plate 6

Ice-pail and cover; soft-paste
porcelain, painted in enamel
colours
Mark: anchor in red enamel
CHELSEA; c.1755
Height 6 ins.

Private Collection

Among the many styles of Meissen decorations which were imitated by
the Chelsea painters, was their naturalistic flower painting, the *deutsche
Blumen*. Once again the Chelsea workmen were able to copy directly from
the collection of Sir Charles Hanbury Williams, and in many instances the
painting is so similar that, when viewed through a glass case, it is very
difficult to separate the wares of the two factories.

Chelsea table-ware can often be distinguished by the three or four minor
blemishes in the glaze on the base which are termed 'spur marks'. These
were caused by the practice of using fire-clay supports beneath the pieces in
the kiln during the second firing, when it was necessary to prevent the fluid
glaze from fusing to the inside of the fireclay saggar. It then often became
necessary to grind away any surplus glaze which accumulated on the foot
rim, giving the further distinctive feature of a ground foot rim, which also
provides a good opportunity to feel the smooth soft-paste free of glaze.

When held before a strong light the Chelsea porcelain of this period
often shows bright spots of clearer translucency. These 'moons', as they are
called, were once thought to have been caused by the glassy 'frit' in the
paste, but are now known to be the result of minute pockets of air being
trapped in the clay.

Plate 7

Plate; soft-paste porcelain,
decorated with 'Mazarin' blue and
enamel colours
Mark: anchor in gold
CHELSEA; 1760–65
Diameter 9 ins.

Private Collection

From about 1758 both the glaze and the composition of the Chelsea paste
underwent changes. Bone-ash, which had been used at the Bow factory
since its establishment, was included and a thicker 'juicy' glaze, which was
very inclined to 'craze', was also adopted. These two changes cannot be
considered an improvement, and often resulted in the wares becoming
badly stained.

The plate illustrated bears what is usually referred to as the Mecklenburg
pattern. In 1763 George III and Queen Charlotte presented her brother, the
Duke of Mecklenburg-Strelitz, with a very large and costly service, which
included an épergne, candlesticks, salt-cellars, etc. Chelsea then advertised
similarly decorated wares as 'the same as the Royal Pattern which was sold
for 1150 pounds'. From this time it became very evident that Chelsea were
seeking to imitate the more fashionable styles popularised by the French
factory of Sèvres. In 1770 the Chelsea factory was taken over by William
Duesbury, proprietor of the Derby concern, and production continued
until 1784. This period is referred to as 'Chelsea-Derby', and is discussed
under Derby.

Plate 8

Figure of a man, symbolic of
'smell' from a set of The Five
Senses; white glazed porcelain
DERBY; c.1750–55
Height 7 ins.

As with many other 18th-century English porcelain factories, there is still
some doubt as to exactly when the material was first manufactured at
Derby. The earliest dated examples are three very rare, but poorly potted,
jugs, inscribed 'D. 1750', 'Derby' and 'D'.

The potter responsible was almost certainly Andrew Planché, who
presumably learnt the secrets of the manufacture on the Continent prior to
his arrival in this country. There seems every reason to suppose that the
wares were produced at the china manufactory of 'Mr. Heath and
Company', near St. Mary's Bridge, Derby, and not the Cockpit Hill
creamware factory as previously suggested. There are over fifty different
models associated with this family, most of which are left in the white
glazed state. Some of the figures have had enamel colours added by
William Duesbury, whose London account books of 1751–53 record the
decoration of 'Darby' and 'Darbishire figures'.

Apart from the set, The Five Senses, other models include The Four
Seasons, The Elements, various classical figures, and animals such as boars,
stags, bulls and birds. These figures often show certain common
characteristics, for example, they are always slip-cast, the glaze, which is
very white, invariably stops short of the edge of the base and the hole in
the base, which provides an escape for the air trapped in the interior of the
hollow figure during firing, is often of a form referred to as a 'screw hole'
(because it looks as though it could have been reamed out to house a
countersunk screw).

Plate 9

Vase; soft-paste porcelain, decorated with enamel colours
DERBY; 1756–60 Height 10¼ ins.

In 1756 the premises which had been occupied by Heath and Company
were extended by the acquisition of some adjacent properties. An
agreement for January 1st, 1756, named 'John Heath of Derby . . .
Gentleman . . . Andrew Planché of the same place, China Maker . . . and
Wm. Duesbury of Longton, Enamellor' as partners. This agreement was
never executed, and later documents suggest that Planché never became a
partner in the concern.

Due to a lack of documentary evidence it is difficult to attribute wares to
the early years of W. Duesbury and Company. Some figures of the
1756–60 period certainly bear a close resemblance to the earlier Planché
modelling, so there is a likelihood that Planché did continue to work for
Duesbury for a period.

This handsome vase of Chinese form is perhaps preferable to many of
the contemporary Derby vases of extreme rococo form. The flower
painting is very much in the Meissen style, but the vignettes of figures are a
good pointer to early Duesbury Derby of the 'pale-coloured' family,
which were so often spoilt by a heavily-blued glaze.

Private Collection

Plate 10

Plate; soft-paste porcelain, painted
in underglaze-blue
DERBY; *c*.1760
Diameter 8¾ ins.

Despite the fact that porcelain
decorated with underglaze-blue
could be produced much more
cheaply than enamelled wares,
Duesbury made comparatively
few examples of this type,
doubtless preferring to try and
match the finer productions of the
rival Chelsea factory. The plate
shown is typical of the limited
range of jugs, sauce-boats, baskets,
pot-pourri and plates made prior to
c.1770. They are all rather fussily
decorated, compared with either
Bow or Worcester, probably in
order to justify higher prices.
Many of these useful wares show

Formerly Gilbert Bradley Collection

the same characteristic Derby 'patch marks', as discussed on page 22. The
underglaze-blue, derived from the metallic oxide of cobalt, is particularly
bright and vivid on most early Derby wares, and usually shows a distinct
purple tone emphasised by the very white paste which shows the same
distinctive 'moons' of clearer translucency as Chelsea of the 'red-anchor'
period.

Plate 11

The Four Seasons; soft-paste
porcelain, painted in enamel
colours
DERBY; 1760–65 Height 6¼ ins.

Constance and Anthony Chiswell Antiques

For many years large numbers of
unmarked Derby figures were
thought to have been produced at
either Chelsea or Bow, until
eventually a common feature on
all these pieces was noticed by the
late Bernard Rackham, a former
Keeper of the Department of
Ceramics at the Victoria and
Albert Museum. It was noticed
that all these unmarked examples,
and later well-authenticated pieces
of Derby, had three or four dark
unglazed patches on the base. This
was the result of supporting the wares on small pads of clay during the
glaze firing. These 'patch marks' can be seen on both unmarked pieces
and those with incised numbers tallying with the later Derby price list.

Colours can also be used to help one arrive at a correct attribution, in
this instance the figure symbolic of 'Spring', on the left of the group,
clearly shows the early 'dirty turquoise', which was inclined to fire to a
brownish tone.

Plate 12

Two figures representing David
Garrick as Tancred, and a female
street-seller; soft-paste porcelain,
painted in enamel colours
DERBY; c.1765 Height 10 ins.

The English porcelain factories not
only imitated the Italian Comedy
figures of Harlequin and his fellow
characters, as portrayed by
Kaendler, the Meissen modeller,
but in many instances set a new
fashion by depicting well-known
actors and actresses of the period,
in roles they made famous. The
male figure shown here is known
to represent David Garrick as
Tancred, a part he first played in
1744–45 in Thompson's *Tancred
and Sigismunda*. The female figure
shown alongside has for many
years been accepted as Mrs Cibber,
the actress, playing the part of a

Constance and Anthony Chiswell Antiques

Vivandière. In *English Porcelain Figures of the Eighteenth Century*, the late Arthur Lane suggests that these figures are entirely unrelated and the female character is a street-seller.

The enamel decoration of this period has much in common with that on contemporary figures of the Chelsea 'gold-anchor' period. From about 1758 the Derby factory had seemingly realised that the early over-blued glaze did little to improve their figures and it was replaced with a good colourless glaze, which showed the creamy-white porcelain to advantage.

Constance and Anthony Chiswell Antiques

Plate 13

Figure of David Garrick in the role of Richard III
CHELSEA-DERBY; *c.*1775
Height 8¾ ins.

In 1770 the London factory of Chelsea was purchased by William Duesbury and continued under his direction until it eventually closed in 1784.

This particularly fine example of Derby 'biscuit' porcelain can best be described from the Chelsea-Derby Sale Catalogue for 9th February, 1773, where what was almost certainly a similar example was entered as 'A fine figure of Garrick in the character of Richard the Third, in biscuit, 1*l*.10*s*.'. The figure is No. 21 in the Derby price list where the modelling is attributed to John Bacon, R.A, but there seems little foundation for this. The original painting of Garrick in this role was first exhibited by Nathaniel Dance at the Royal Academy in 1771. The figure was undoubtedly modelled from an engraving by J. Dixon of Dance's painting.

Plate 15

Basket; soft-paste porcelain,
painted in enamel colours
Mark: gilt anchor and D
monogram
DERBY; 1770–84
Length 9¼ ins.

From about 1770 William
Duesbury began to produce a
porcelain body with a high
percentage of bone-ash (calcined
animal bone). This enabled him to
produce a wide range of table-
wares which number among the
most pleasing and practical of
18th-century English porcelains.

The basket shown is decorated
with very typical scattered sprays
of flowers, a style of decoration
also used at Worcester over this

Plate 14

Three Graces distressing Cupid; decorated with enamel colours
Mark: N.235 incised
CHELSEA-DERBY; late-18th century
Height 17¼ ins.

This group of Three Graces distressing Cupid is from an engraving
(*Etiam Amor Criminibus Plectitur*) by William Wynne Ryland after a
painting entitled *Three Nymphs Distressing Cupid* by Angelica Kauffmann.
The model appears in two sizes in the 'price list' published by John
Haslem in *The Old Derby China Factory* (1876) but, unfortunately, this list
is undated.

Many of the larger groups produced by Duesbury in the Chelsea-
Derby period were adopted from those originated at such Continental
factories as Meissen, Tournai or Sèvres. The fashion of leaving groups 'in
the biscuit' was first introduced, in about 1751, at Vincennes' a factory
whose fine soft-paste was far more suitable for this purpose than the
rather coarse and easily-stained material of Derby at that period.

It is interesting to note that this same group would be more expensive
when unglazed in the white than fully decorated as illustrated. This was
because only few pieces emerged from the first firing in a perfect
condition. Glaze and decoration were often used to disguise minor repairs
and blemishes.

period. Other popular designs followed the trend towards neo-Classical
styles, which included classical urns or portrait-busts of classical figures
coupled with swags, garlands and ribbons. Little is known of the work of
the individual painters at this period, but Richard Askew is credited with
the painting of robust little cupids among clouds, usually painted in
crimson monochrome and obviously inspired by the slightly earlier
decoration seen on Sèvres porcelain.

Plate 16

Figures of a nun and a monk; soft-paste porcelain, painted with enamel colours
CHELSEA-DERBY; 1770–84
Heights 6¾ ins. and 7 ins.

Figures of monks and nuns were particularly popular during the Chelsea-Derby period and were invariably supported on the newly introduced rock-like bases, picked out in pale green and salmon-pink. Haslem's list notes *Nos. 102–113 Twelve Figures of Nuns and Monks*. Many of the figures of this period are the work of Pierre Stephan, who was engaged as a modeller in 1770.

Plate 17

Ice-pail; soft-paste porcelain, decorated with enamel colours and gilding
Mark: crown, crossed batons and 'D' in red enamel
DERBY; early-19th century
Height 9¾ ins.

John Warrell Collection

Following the death of William Duesbury in 1786 the factory was continued by his son, William Duesbury II, who, two years prior to his own death in 1797 took an Irish miniature painter, Michael Kean, into partnership. Kean continued to run the factory until 1811. The business then appears to have been managed by Robert Bloor, who eventually took over the lease of the concern in 1815. The responsibility was apparently so great that, in 1828, Bloor went insane, although his name continued to be associated with the factory until its closure in 1848.

It was during these years that Derby produced a mass of finely decorated porcelain associated with such well-known names as Zachariah Boreman, William Billingsley, 'Jockey' Hill (who rode to work on horseback), Richard Askew, James Banford, William 'Quaker' Pegg, George Robertson and Robert and John Brewer. The ice-pail shown, which has an inner liner to contain the dessert, is decorated with landscape painting of a style considered to be that of George Robertson, who produced a great many similar landscapes between 1795 and 1820, always very much in the style of the oil-painting of the period, and usually in autumnal tints.

Plate 18

Figure of a peacock; bone-china,
painted in enamel colours and gilt
Mark: 'DERBY' on a ribbon
beneath a crown
DERBY; *c.*1830
Height 6½ ins.

This figure of a peacock proved to be so popular that it was produced
from about 1830 until the closure of the factory in 1848, and was then
re-issued by the present Royal Crown Derby Porcelain Co. Ltd., which
was not established until 1876.

In addition to the price list published by Haslem, he notes a further list
of eighteen figures, including 'Peacock among Flowers', which are all
considered to be by John Whitaker, who was working at Derby from
1818. This modeller was manager of the ornamental department from
1830 until the works closed in 1848, when he went to work for Minton
in Staffordshire.

27

Anthony Chiswell Collection

Plate 19

Two figures of dwarfs; soft-paste
porcelain, painted in enamel
colours
DERBY; *c.*1820
Height 7 ins.

These well-known Derby dwarfs were first mentioned in the factory's
sale catalogues of 1784 as 'grotesque Punches'. They proved so popular
that they were produced throughout the remaining life of the factory and
were later re-issued by the present-day Derby concern. Reproductions
have also been made on the Continent in a hard-paste porcelain.

The figure on the left is the same model as produced at Chelsea from
about 1752. Both are based on the original set of twenty engravings by
Jacques Callot, first published in 1616 (*Varie figure gobbi*). These Derby
versions are more popularly known today as 'The Mansion House
Dwarfs', because of the practice of the Derby painters of adding
advertising matter to the hats, such as was worn by actual dwarfs
engaged to stand in the area of the Mansion House in London,
forerunners of the present-day 'sandwich-board' men.

Plate 20

Finger-bowl stand; bone-porcelain, painted in underglaze-blue
Mark: letter 'R' incised
BOW; *c.*1752
Diameter 5¾ ins.

Formerly Gilbert Bradley Collection

The actual site of the Bow factory is now known to have been on the Essex side of the River Lea, although the early experiments of 1744–49 were probably conducted in buildings in nearby Bow. The first early patent of 1744 granted to Thomas Frye and Edward Heylyn, was concerned with the manufacture of the material for the making of porcelain, and not with the production of actual wares. It was not until 1749 that a further patent was enrolled which claimed the manufacture of wares comparable to those being imported from the Far East. As these were fine, hard-paste porcelain this was a rash claim.

A soft-paste porcelain, which contained bone-ash, was probably being produced in commercial quantities by 1747, financed by a certain wealthy Alderman Arnold (*d.*1751). Their early wares were either left in the white glazed condition, or decorated with underglaze-blue painting, often in the fashion of the imported Chinese porcelain of that period. Enamel colours were unlikely to have been used at the factory before 1750. We know that William Duesbury was adding colours to Bow figures between 1751–53.

Bow, unlike Chelsea, aimed to cater for the less wealthy customer, and in its early years had very large sales, necessitating the opening of a warehouse in Cornhill, London. Among the earliest dated pieces of Bow is an inkpot inscribed 'Made at New Canton 1750', so named because 'the model of the building was taken from that of Canton in China'. This finger-bowl stand shows all the characteristics of early Bow, the body is well-fired and shows a dirty-white translucency when held before an artificial light and the glaze seems to have been underfired in order to prevent it becoming too fluid thus spoiling the crispness of the underglaze-blue painting. These early pieces were often incised with a letter 'R', presumably a workman's mark. No regular factory-marks were used at this period.

Plate 21

Dish: soft-paste porcelain, decorated
with applied reliefs of plum-
blossom and enamel decoration
BOW; 1750–55
Length 10¾ ins.

Dated examples from 1750 provide the necessary evidence for suggesting
that from this time enamel colours were being used at the Bow factory. It
is only on very rare occasions that any knowledge concerning enamel
decoration can be learnt from 'wasters' found on the site of an early
factory. If any wares had successfully survived the 'biscuit' and 'glost'
kilns, the fusing of the enamel colours at the comparatively low
temperature of about 800°C was a fairly simple operation which only
rarely went wrong.

Many fragments were found on the Bow site with sprays of applied
plum-blossom, imitating the so-called 'prunus', seen on so much of
the exported porcelain made in the Fukien province of China
(*blanc-de-Chine*) from the 17th century onwards.

The dish illustrated shows not only the popular relief plum-blossom,
but a particularly attractive style of enamel decoration used at Bow from
the early 1750's, this is *famille rose*. The term *famille rose* is used to indicate
any style of Chinese porcelain decoration which, from the early-18th
century, included a rose-coloured enamel which could be tinted with
white to produce a variety of hues ranging from a pale pink to a deep
crimson. This colour is thought to have first been used by late-17th
century German enamellers, the colour being derived from chloride of
gold.

Plate 22

Dish; soft-paste porcelain, painted
with enamel colours in the
'Kakiemon' style
BOW; 1750–55
Diameter 9 ins.

It was during the middle decades of the 17th century that, due to internal
strife in China, the Dutch East India Company turned to Japan as an
alternative source of supply for Oriental porcelain. In this way Europe
became conversant with Arita porcelain and grew to particularly
appreciate that which was decorated in the so-called 'Kakiemon' fashion,
the nickname given to a Japanese potter said to have introduced the
particular style of painting illustrated on this octagonal dish.

In documents concerned with the day-to-day running of the Bow
factory in 1756, one reads of '*parteridge octogon plates*'. This is only one of
a whole variety of subjects painted in the Kakiemon style at Bow.
Probably due to the fact that the Bow decorators were less skilled than
those employed at Chelsea, their rendering of these Japanese patterns
captures the free and careless manner of the originals more than any of
the other contemporary factories, such as Chelsea, Meissen or Chantilly,
who also decorated much of their porcelain in this same fashion.

Plate 23

Figure of Jupiter; soft-paste porcelain, painted in enamel colours
BOW; *c.*1755
Height 6½ ins.

Many of the figures made at Bow up until about 1755 show a distinct 'family likeness' in facial features, which suggests the work of a single modeller. The figures were rarely original and have nearly all been traced to either Meissen or engravings. Bow produced their figures by pressing the prepared 'sheets' of clay into the walls of the plaster moulds, a process referred to as 'press-moulding', which usually resulted in their figures being rather heavier than those of Chelsea or Derby. Probably the best examples of this period are the 'Nine Muses', all of whom, appropriately, look like sisters.

From about 1754 Bow figures were only rarely left 'in the white' and the work of a new and more competent modeller was apparent. The enamel colours used at Bow are often a sure guide to attribution, the opaque light blue, seen on the cloak of Jupiter, being very typical. Use was also made of a deep crimson and a very transparent emerald green which was at times applied so thickly that 'tears' were often formed. In *English Porcelain Figures of the 18th Century*, the late Arthur Lane likens such models as this to the work of the Italian sculptor Bernini.

Private Collection

Plate 24

Pair of figures, a girl with a lamb and a boy with a dog; soft-paste porcelain, painted in enamel colours
Marks: an anchor and dagger in red enamel
BOW; 1765–70
Heights 6½ ins. and 6¾ ins.

This pair of later Bow figures shows the typical rococo bases adopted by the factory from about 1759, a style that did little to improve the figures. The majority of these Bow pedestals were of a distinct table-like form with four 'S' scroll feet, usually picked out in underglaze-blue and crimson enamel, or the more 'Chelsea-like' gilding as shown.

From about 1763 Bow figures and useful wares were often painted with the mark of an anchor and a dagger in red enamel. This mark is also often seen on Continental hard-paste reproductions made during the second half of the 19th century. Some of the people responsible for these 'fakes' were obviously a little confused about English factory marks and reproductions of some Bow models were at times marked with a Chelsea version of a 'gold anchor'.

Plate 25

Jug; soft-paste porcelain, painted
in underglaze-blue
Mark: Number '3' on inside of
foot-rim in underglaze-blue
LOWESTOFT; 1765–70
Height 8½ ins.

Formerly Gilbert Bradley Collection

The old term 'Chinese-Lowestoft' is one that is rarely heard today and it
is now generally appreciated that there was no connection whatsoever
between the hard-paste porcelain of China, and the charming soft-paste
porcelain wares of the small factory of Lowestoft in East Anglia.

This particularly fine jug is traditionally considered to have once been
in the possession of Robert Browne, the manager and one of the most
important of the four original partners who established the factory in
1760. It was obviously not the aim of the concern to compete with such
contemporary factories as Chelsea, Bow, Derby or Worcester, and,
although Lowestoft was concerned with a china warehouse in London
for a period during the 1770s, it seemed to cater primarily for local
demand.

Up until the time of Robert Browne's death in 1771, the only painted
decoration used at Lowestoft consisted of the fashionable underglaze-
blue. The earliest productions were of a poor quality bone porcelain,
sparsely decorated with rather misunderstood *chinoiserie* patterns applied
in a rather inky-blue. Wares with relief-moulded decoration date from
about 1760, and today are usually attributed to the modeller James
Hughes, whose initials 'I.H.' appear on a number of similarly moulded
examples. Whilst there is at present no actual proof for this attribution
the name is commonly used by collectors to indicate a style of moulding
peculiar to the Lowestoft factory. Collectors should pay attention to the
form of this very characteristic handle, with the 'thumb-rest' and
protruding 'kick', features seen on so many of this factory's wares.

Plate 27

Group of small animals; soft-paste
porcelain, painted with enamel
colours
LOWESTOFT; late-18th century
Heights 1½–2 ins.

Plate 26

Mug; soft-paste porcelain, painted in enamel colours by the 'Tulip painter'
LOWESTOFT; *c*.1775
Height 5½ ins.

From about 1768 the proprietors of Lowestoft decided to make many of
their wares more attractive with the addition of enamel colours, apart
from their continued range of pieces decorated with painted, or printed
underglaze-blue. Among the most sought-after of these enamelled pieces
are those vaguely attributed to the 'Tulip-painter', who, in addition to
painting rather blowsy tulips, also painted other varieties of flowers, as
shown. The general simplicity of style so often apparent in Lowestoft is
well illustrated here in the soft-coloured sprawling flowers, which bear
no relation to the form of the vessel. The painting is rather reminiscent of
that seen on Marseilles faience, where the flowers appear to have been
carelessly tossed onto the surface. This painter's hand can at times be
identified on Lowestoft porcelain decorated with flowers in a single
enamel, usually pink.

These figures had, until recently, been attributed to the earlier factory of
Longton Hall in Staffordshire, but finds in the form of 'wasters' on the
site of the factory have enabled certain small models of cats, dogs, swans,
etc., to be attributed to Lowestoft. The little tabby-cat is well
documented as there is an original mould in a private collection from
which identical cats were cast. The seated dog, in typical Lowestoft
colours, helps to identify other identical models of dogs decorated in
underglaze purple, a colour derived from manganese. The two
differently enamelled swans illustrated are both equally rare. All these
small animals also have certain characteristics in common, for example,
the bases are always glazed over and the air-hole is of a similar funnel
shape to that of early Derby figures.

    As a result of competition from cheaper yet more refined earthenware,
and the more lavishly decorated porcelain being made at such factories as
Worcester and Derby, the trade of Lowestoft declined and production
appears to have come to an end about 1801.

Plate 28

Cup and saucer; soft-paste
porcelain, painted in underglaze-
blue
LONGTON HALL; c.1755
Diameter of saucer 4½ ins.

Formerly Gilbert Bradley Collection

Since about the middle of the 17th century Staffordshire had been
recognised as the centre of the English pottery industry, but the potters in
that area were apparently so steeped in the manufacture of their
traditional earthenware and stoneware that they were adverse to
experimenting with the new and popular material of porcelain. The
exceptional factories in this respect being the Pomona at Newcastle (see
page 9) and that at Longton Hall, established by William Jenkinson in
1749, and brought to a close in 1760 by the Rev. Charlesworth.

William Littler, whose name had long been associated with the
Longton Hall factory, was first a partner and later manager. He
apparently had the necessary technical knowledge, which he may well
have acquired by working in London, but he lacked the necessary
finance. Littler's name is used to describe a very brilliant blue, which was
used to imitate the ground-colour of Chelsea and Sèvres, although rather
unsuccessfully as it was inclined to run badly, a fact which resulted in
there being many unfinished wasters.

The early wares of Longton Hall were rather primitive and made in a
clumsy fashion which was entirely unsuitable for practical table-wares,
but this fault was overcome by about 1754. Apart from large numbers of
naturalistically moulded and coloured wares, such as sauce-boats and
tureens in the form of cos lettuce, strawberry-leaf dishes, tulip-cups and
bowls, and melon tureens, many cups, saucers, small jugs, mugs and
teapots were produced, painted in a greyish-blue of a somewhat similar
tone to that on early Worcester wares. This 'prunus-root' pattern is one
of several patterns first introduced at the Worcester factory.

Plate 29

Group of putti feeding a goat with
grapes; soft-paste porcelain,
painted with enamel colours
LONGTON HALL; 1756–57
Height $4\frac{1}{2}$ ins.

Private Collection

The early white figures produced at Longton Hall are appropriately
referred to as the 'Snowman' group, which consists of a whole variety of
birds, horses, cows, sheep and extremely primitive figures from Chinese
and Meissen originals. This group of putti feeding a goat with flowers
could well have been intended to symbolise Spring. The Staffordshire
modellers appear to have found it difficult to adapt their skill to the more
sophisticated material of porcelain, especially when coupled with the new
fashion for rococo, as can clearly be seen here. This same group also well
illustrates the characteristic palette, including a pinkish-crimson and a
pale yellow-green, of many later Longton Hall figures. The moulds used
for this model were apparently used again at the later hard-paste
porcelain factory of William Cookworthy, which was established at
Plymouth in 1768.

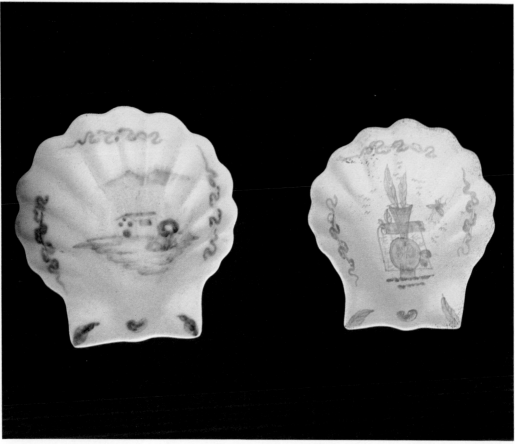

Plate 30

Pair of pickle-trays; soapstone porcelain, painted in underglaze-blue.
LIVERPOOL (William Reid's factory); 1755–61
Length $4\frac{1}{4}$ and $3\frac{3}{8}$ ins.

It was only during recent years that ceramic specialists have endeavoured to attribute the porcelain made at Liverpool during the second half of the 18th century to specific factories or groups. Up until 1755 the Liverpool pottery of Richard Chaffers had been engaged in the manufacture of earthenware, but from the time they learnt the secret of the manufacture of soapstone porcelain, from Richard Podmore a renegade workman from the Worcester factory, they produced some excellent wares decorated in either underglaze-blue or enamel colours. Similar wares were produced by Chaffers's successor, Philip Christian, who continued to run the factory until 1776.

These two pickle-trays are attributed to a further Liverpool factory, that of William Reid, known as the Liverpool China Manufactory. Reid was probably making porcelain similar to that of Chaffers by 1755, but was unfortunately forced to close through his bankruptcy in 1761. At the time of writing many such Liverpool wares are subject to differences of opinion among collectors.

37

Plate 31

Punch-pot; soft-paste porcelain, decorated with underglaze-blue painting
Mark: incised workman's mark (as a reversed number 3)
WORCESTER; c.1754
Height 7¾ ins.

Formerly Gilbert Bradley Collection

The wares made by Benjamin Lund and William Miller at Bristol from about 1748–52 are difficult to separate from those produced at Worcester during their early years. There seems very little doubt that the famous Dr. Wall and his fourteen original partners, who were responsible for the establishment of the Worcester Tonquin Manufacture in 1751, fully intended at the time to take over the Bristol concern in order to acquire the knowledge appertaining to the manufacture of a superior type of soft-paste porcelain. This porcelain, thought by some to be nearer a hard-paste, included a high proportion of soaprock, which was quarried under licence in the area of the Lizard Peninsula in Cornwall.

Recent excavations on the site of the early Worcester factory, Warmstry House, have revealed that many wares, which in the past have been attributed solely to the early Bristol concern, were in fact also made at Worcester. A few marked sauce-boats, cream-boats and figures of Chinese deities actually have the word 'Bristoll' moulded in relief.

In his book *English Blue and White Porcelain*, Dr. Bernard Watney has enabled the collector to recognise certain patterns of both painted and printed underglaze-blue decoration associated with the various factories. The so-called 'zig-zag fence pattern' which was very popular on early Worcester, is painted here on a rare and exceptionally large teapot-shaped vessel, which was intended for serving punch rather than the costly tea.

Formerly Gilbert Bradley Collection

Plate 32

Vase, one of a garniture of five; soft-paste porcelain, decorated in underglaze-blue
WORCESTER; 1755–60
Height 7¾ ins.

The first potters to produce sets of five vases for the decoration of high chimney-pieces were almost certainly the Dutch, who monopolised the porcelain trade with the Far East during the 17th century. Through this contact the Chinese in turn began to make similar blue-and-white porcelain garnitures for export to Europe. These sets of vases, two as illustrated and three of baluster form with covers, became very popular in England and were imitated a great deal, but nowhere more so than at Worcester. The elongated Chinese lady is referred to by the Dutch expression of *lange lijzen*, which actually translates to 'long stupid', and not 'long Eliza' as so often suggested.

From about 1760 Worcester began to use several different factory-marks (among them the well-known crescent) either painted or printed, usually according to the type of decoration being applied at the time. There are, of course, always the odd exceptions to these generalisations.

Plate 33

Large leaf-shape dish; porcelain,
enamel and gilt decoration
WORCESTER; 1765–70
Length 12½ ins.

In the late 1760s Worcester decorated many of their wares in various
patterns inspired by Chinese and Japanese porcelain. Sometimes these
designs were almost exact reproductions of the originals, others are more
fanciful interpretations. Judging by the mid–18th-century catalogue
references all Japanese porcelain must at that time have been thought to
be of considerable age, for they write of 'old mosaick Japan', 'fine old
Japan fan pattern', 'fine old rich dragon pattern', etc.

Plate 34

Dish; soft-paste porcelain, moulded in relief, decorated in enamel colours
WORCESTER; *c.*1765
Diameter $5\frac{1}{4}$ ins.

There must be very few English porcelain collectors who have not heard
of the 'blind Earl' pattern. This pattern was normally used on small dishes
moulded in relief with rose-leaf and buds, a design which has remained so
popular that it is still produced in bone-china by the present Worcester
porcelain company. The term 'blind Earl' is a little misleading as to date,
for the name refers to the Earl of Coventry, who did not go blind until
1780, whilst the pattern was certainly being produced during the 1760's.

The most common versions of the 'blind Earl' are decorated in
underglaze-blue, which is used to 'pick-out' the moulded reliefs. In other
varieties the leaf and bud motif is completely ignored and overpainted
with unrelated styles of enamel painting or printed decoration, but this
can at times be equally attractive, as shown on this example.

Constance and Anthony Chiswell Antiques

Plate 35

Teapot; soft-paste porcelain,
decorated in enamel colours
WORCESTER; 1760–65
Height $4\frac{1}{2}$ ins.

Many of the teapots made at the
various English porcelain factories
during the third quarter of the
18th century, were fashioned after
those being imported from China
during the same period. This
Worcester example of 'Mandarin
porcelain' is typical, but it will be
noticed that the spout curves,
whereas the majority of the Far
Eastern teapots have a straight
spout. In addition this version has a
typical Worcester flower-knop.

Constance and Anthony Chiswell Antiques

41

Plate 36

Teapot; soft-paste porcelain,
painted in enamel colours
WORCESTER; *c.*1770
Height 5½ ins.

By about 1768 the Worcester proprietors were employing painters who
had previously been employed by Nicholas Sprimont, at the Chelsea
factory in London. From this time Worcester began to produce more
lavishly decorated wares which equalled, and often surpassed, those made
at Chelsea during the 'gold anchor' period, thus justifying their claim
that 'any orders will be executed in the highest taste and much cheaper
than can be afforded by any painters in London'.

This teapot shows the beauty of the famous Worcester 'apple-green', a
term which appears to be a more recent trade name. In the 1769
announcement of a public auction sale of Worcester wares, mention was
made of many colours including sea-green, French-green and pea-green
and the colour shown is almost certainly the latter. Difficulty was
apparently experienced in fusing the gilding to this particular colour, for
it will be noticed that the gilt scrollwork lies alongside the green enamel,
and not astride it as was more customary. It was at this same time that
many wares were being made at Worcester with the well-known scale-
blue ground, a style that has been reproduced a great deal on hard-paste
porcelain over recent years, especially by the firm of Samson in France.

Plate 37

Tureen; porcelain, painted in
enamel colours and gilt, with a
picture of Colchester Castle,
Essex
Mark: crown and 'B.F.B'
impressed
WORCESTER (Barr, Flight
and Barr); 1807–13
Height 6½ ins.

John Warrell Collection

Worcester is the only English porcelain factory that has continued in
production from its start in 1751, until the present day. Dr. Wall, one of
the original partners died in 1776, and collectors now refer to objects
made prior to that date as being of the 'Wall period'. The factory was
continued under the management of William Davis, the chemist of the
concern, until 1783, when the factory was purchased by John Flight, the
firm's London agent, for his two sons. The years from 1776–93 are now
referred to by the trade and collectors as the 'Davis & Flight period'. It
was during this period that some very poor quality blue-and-white
printed wares were produced.

Flight then took Martin Barr into partnership and the factory
continued as the 'Flight & Barr' concern until 1807. It was following this
partnership, during the 'Barr, Flight & Barr' management (1807–13) that
this very attractive tureen was produced. From 1813 a further change of
partnership resulted in the 'Flight, Barr & Barr' period, lasting until 1840,
when the factory was taken over by the more successful concern of
Chamberlain. Worcester porcelain of these periods can usually be easily
identified by the very full and self-explanatory marks which they used.

Plate 38

Mug; bone-china, painted in
enamel colours and gilt
Mark: Grainger, Lee and Co.
WORCESTER (Grainger,
Lee & Co); 1812–39
Height 4½ ins.

Thomas Grainger first established his porcelain factory at Worcester in
1800, taking his brother-in-law, a Mr. Lee, into partnership in about
1812. The firm continued under the name of 'Grainger, Lee & Co.' until
Lee retired in about 1839. The factory was continued by the family until
it was incorporated with the Royal Worcester Porcelain Company in
1889, and was eventually closed in 1902.

The Grainger, Lee wares were of an excellent quality, and much of
their output was marketed by John Mortlock, the outstanding London
ceramic retailer of the 19th century, continuing in business until about
1930. The mug illustrated, with its painting of a stage-coach, is a
particularly pleasing example and is of greater interest than many of the
wares produced by this firm.

Constance and Anthony Chiswell Antiques

Plate 39

Coffee-can and saucer; bone-china, decorated with enamel colours and gilt
Mark: Chamberlain's Worcester WORCESTER (Chamberlain's factory); *c.*1820
Diameter (of saucer) $5\frac{1}{4}$ ins.

In about 1786 Robert Chamberlain left the main Worcester factory, where he was apprenticed, to start up on his own account as a decorator, mainly for the Caughley wares of Thomas Turner. (See Plate 42.)

From about 1790 he began to produce wares on his own account, and was, in fact, so successful that in 1840 new buildings were erected on the Chamberlain site and his works were combined with those of Flight, Barr & Barr. It is surprising to find the mark of Chamberlain on such a modestly decorated coffee-can. Tea and coffee services were often combined, with a single saucer being made for use with either a teacup or a coffee-can. This particular form of handle, with the small protruding 'spur' is a form seen on many of the wares produced by the Chamberlain concern.

45

Plate 40

Plate; bone-china, painted in
enamel colours and gilt
Mark: Patent Office registration
mark for January 14th, 1880 and
the standard printed trade-mark
of the Royal Worcester factory
WORCESTER; dated 1880
Diameter 9½ ins.

From 1840–52 the Worcester porcelain factory enjoyed twelve
prosperous years under the direction of the Chamberlains. The factory
was then conducted by W. H. Kerr and R. W. Binns, who aimed to
introduce completely new forms and styles of decoration, rather than to
revive and improve on the old. It was during the Kerr & Binns period
that Thomas Bott executed so much of his fine painting in the fashion of
the earlier Limoges enamels of France. These examples, and others made
during the comparatively short period of Kerr & Binns, are greatly in
demand amongst modern collectors and can easily be recognised by their
recorded marks.

The Worcester Royal Porcelain Company was established in 1862 and
several of the painters of the Kerr & Binns period continued to produce
similar work for the new company. The design of this well-painted plate
was first registered with the Patent Office on January 14th, 1880. The
numbers and letters in each corner of the 'diamond mark' enable one to
check by the Patent Office class index, which particular firm had taken
the precaution of registering the design against 'piracy', a patent which
held good for a period of three years. This system was introduced in 1842
and gives the earliest possible date, but a popular design was sometimes
kept in production for a much longer period, still bearing the original
date mark. The 'diamond mark' was abandoned in 1883 and replaced the
following year with a simple sequence of consecutive numbers, which by
1900 had reached 351202.

Constance and Anthony Chiswell Antiques

Plate 41

Six asparagus servers, with
butter-dish (?); decorated in
underglaze-blue
CAUGHLEY; c.1785 (the dish is
Worcester)
Length 3 ins.

Caughley (pronounced Calf-ley) is some two miles south of Broseley in
Shropshire. A pottery had probably existed here since about 1750, but it
was in 1772 that Thomas Turner (1749–1809), who had trained as an
engraver at the Worcester porcelain company, moved to Caughley to
start manufacturing a soapstone porcelain of an almost identical body to
that already being produced at Worcester and Liverpool.

Up until 1964 there had been a great deal of confusion among
collectors over the productions of Caughley and Worcester during the
last quarter of the 18th century. Many wares with rather inferior transfer-
printed decoration had for many years been wrongly attributed to
Caughley, especially those bearing a number from one to nine, drawn as
a Chinese character. Excavations, which became possible at this time,
revealed new and valuable finds in the form of factory 'wasters',
shedding new light on Caughley productions. At about this same time
further excavations also took place on the site of the early Worcester
factory, confirming many theories of local ceramic historians that much
of the 'poor quality Caughley', had in fact been made at Worcester
during the 'Davis & Flight' period (1776–93).

These asparagus servers, probably used to serve individual portions of
this delicacy, are decorated with a pattern referred to as the 'Pleasure
Boat' or 'Fisherman' pattern. This pattern was used at both factories
mentioned and could, with others, well be from the engravings of
Robert Hancock, who also left Worcester for Caughley at about the
same time as Turner. There are slight differences which help
identification, for example, the Caughley fisherman is holding a small fat
fish whilst the Worcester man holds a much longer 'bite', also, the line of
the fisherman above is usually taut on the Caughley version and slack on
the Worcester. A recently discovered jug with the 'S' mark of Caughley,
for 'Salopian', has bewildered collectors by having a slack line, proving
that so many of today's sweeping statements can usually be upset by the
unexpected.

Plate 42

Dessert dish; porcelain decorated
with enamel colours and gilt
Mark: Salopian (impressed)
CAUGHLEY; *c*.1785 (enamel
decoration by Robert
Chamberlain)
Diameter 7 ins.

Over recent years factory records
have been made available by the
present Worcester porcelain
factory which throw fresh light on
a large number of Caughley wares,
which were decorated at Worcester
by Robert Chamberlain.

Flight purchased the Worcester
factory in 1783, shortly after
Chamberlain left his employment
there to start an independent
business, first as an enameller, and
later as a porcelain manufacturer in
his own right. The correspondence
between Thomas Turner and
Chamberlain now prove that a
considerable quantity of Caughley
wares were sent to Worcester to be
decorated with enamel colours and

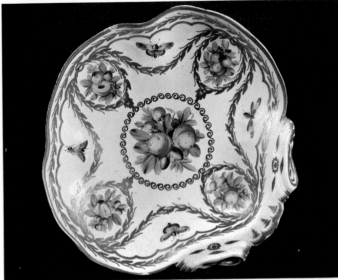

Victoria and Albert Museum

gilding by Chamberlain; some being returned to Caughley and some to
the Caughley warehouse in London, whilst a certain amount was retailed
directly by Chamberlain from his Worcester shop. Trade was obviously
so good that Turner found it difficult to keep up with Chamberlain's
request for undecorated material.

Knowledge of this trade now accounts for the many pieces of
beautifully decorated Caughley, with exceptionally fine enamel and gilt
work such as is shown on this dessert dish. In fact, even this is quite
modest compared with some of his superbly decorated jugs.

Formerly Gilbert Bradley Collection

Plate 43

Plate; hard-paste porcelain,
with underglaze-blue print
Mark: cursive underglaze-blue
device
CAUGHLEY; *c*.1800
Diameter $9\frac{3}{4}$ ins.

Excavation of the Caughley site
helped solve a further collecting
problem. The factory of New Hall
in Staffordshire was producing
wares of a hard-paste porcelain
from 1781 until about 1812, but
there were certain classes of similar
material which the New Hall

collectors would not accept. In his excellent book, *New Hall and Its Imitators*, David Holgate shows a selection of wares now proved, by 'wasters' excavated on the Caughley site, to have been made at this Shropshire factory.

Up until 1796 the New Hall factory management were enjoying the exclusive use, in England, of china-stone and china-clay for the manufacture of a hard-paste porcelain, having purchased from Richard Champion, of the later Bristol factory, his protected patent for the manufacture of true porcelain. From this date, after the patent had expired, these same materials became available to any other potter, although most preferred bone-china, as introduced by Josiah Spode in about 1800. The blue on Caughley hard-paste is much paler.

Plate 44

Miniature ewer; bone-china,
decorated with relief flowers
and enamel painting
Mark: 'C.D' painted in blue
COALPORT; *c.*1825–40
Height 5 ins.

John Rose, who had been apprenticed to Thomas Turner at Caughley, appears to have started the factory of John Rose and Edward Blakeway & Co. at Coalport by about 1796. In 1799 Rose took over the Caughley factory, which he continued to run until about 1814, when the Caughley works were eventually dismantled and Rose's production was continued in the newly enlarged works at Coalport. In about 1926 the concern was moved to Stoke-on-Trent, where wares are still being made today under the name Coalport, but now as a division of the Wedgwood Group.

The alternative name of Coalbrookdale (or Coalbrook Dale) is one commonly associated with the rather ornate wares of the second quarter of the 19th century. This charming little ewer is typical, the 'C.D' (Coalbrookdale) mark leaving no doubt as to the attribution. The collector is warned that some unmarked, but equally attractive, wares were also being made over this period at both the Rockingham works in Yorkshire, and at Mintons in Stoke.

John Warrell Collection

51

Plate 45

Jug; hard-paste porcelain, decorated in underglaze-blue
Mark: the alchemists' sign for tin
PLYMOUTH; 1768–70 Height $3\frac{1}{4}$ ins.

Formerly Gilbert Bradley Collection

Plate 46

Sauce or butter-boat; hard-paste
porcelain, decorated in
underglaze-blue and red enamel
PLYMOUTH; 1768–70
Length 6 ins.

William Cookworthy, a Quaker and a chemist of Plymouth, is known, through contemporary correspondence, to have been interested in the materials necessary for the manufacture of true porcelain as early as the 1740s, but it was not until 1768 that he actually established a factory at Plymouth. There were thirteen shareholders concerned in this venture, including Lord Camelford, upon whose property, near Truro in Cornwall, the materials of china-clay and china-stone were first located in England.

This little blue-and-white jug, or creamer, is typical of the best of their early wares, the blue showing the distinct greyish tint brought about by the high firing temperature required for true porcelain. This seemingly also prevented them from producing such flat-wares as plates and dishes, which were very prone to warping.

The mark used during the company's short stay at Plymouth was the alchemists' sign for tin, looking like a figure '2', with a short upright stroke through the lower horizontal line. After the move to Bristol in 1770, where production continued until 1781, the mark generally used was a simple cross, also sometimes with the letter 'B'.

Constance and Anthony Chiswell Antiques

The early Plymouth wares were more prone to technical faults than those made after the transfer to Bristol in 1770. Difficulty was also experienced, even during the later years at Bristol, in fusing enamel colours on to the hard feldspathic glaze, and they tended to flake off.

Usually the underglaze-blue decoration was deliberately applied in a rather fine pencilled manner, with a weak mixture of the powerful cobalt-blue, but in this instance overfiring and an unusually heavy application of the underglaze-blue has resulted in a near-black blue, but made more attractive here by the additional use of red enamel.

Plate 47

Group of two putti with a goat;
hard-paste porcelain
PLYMOUTH; 1768–70
Height 8½ ins.

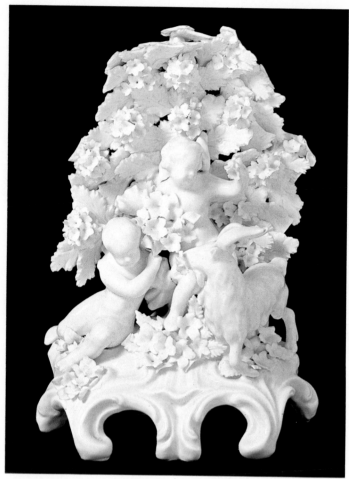

Among the figures attributed to the Plymouth hard-paste porcelain
factory, are some which are basically identical to certain Longton Hall
models. We know that in 1760 about 90,000 pieces of Longton Hall
porcelain were sold at Salisbury in Wiltshire, but there was no mention
made at the time of the sale of equipment or moulds, yet, in some
unaccountable manner, either William Cookworthy or someone
acquainted with him acquired those moulds and used them later to
produce the Plymouth hard-paste porcelain versions. In the example
shown the current porcelain fashion has called for the addition of a *bocage*
(the leaf and flower background).

Plate 48

Sweetmeat dish; hard-paste
porcelain, painted in enamel
colours
Mark: The sign for tin in blue
PLYMOUTH; 1768–70
Diameter 3½ ins.

Private Collection

It is on Plymouth sweetmeat dishes of this form that the letters 'T' or
'To' are sometimes seen and shell salts also seem to have been a particular
favourite form with this workman. The same initials can be seen on
wares of a similar form, made at Bow and Worcester, and are thought to
be those of a 'repairer', a Mr. Tebo (probably Thibaud) about whom
hardly anything is known. The 'repairer' assembled the various sections
of any item made from several different moulds. The colours on this
piece of hard-paste porcelain are considerably brighter than those on the
soft-pastes of other early English factories. There is also a marked
similarity between the bird-painting on this dish and recorded pieces of
the earlier Longton Hall factory.

Formerly Gilbert Bradley Collection

Plate 49

Strainer; hard-paste porcelain, decorated in underglaze-blue
Mark: cross in blue
BRISTOL; c.1775 Diameter 4 ins.

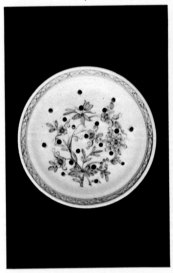

Richard Champion was one of the original shareholders who, in 1774,
took over the full patent rights of the English hard-paste porcelain from
Cookworthy, although he appears to have been mainly responsible for
the running of the factory from about 1772.

Champion carried out many experiments in his endeavours to correct
the various faults he was encountering. He appears to have produced a
glaze which, although feldspathic, was capable of being fused to the
hard-paste body at a slightly lower temperature, resulting in an obvious
improvement in the quality of the underglaze-blue decoration, as
illustrated in this example. Champion was so pleased with this
achievement that in 1779 he advertised: 'The blue and white is now
brought to the greatest perfection equal to the Nankeen, which with the
great Strength and fine Polish [glaze] renders it the best for use of any
China now in the world'; a rather overrated claim.

54

Plate 50

Figure of a girl with a cat and
mousetrap; hard-paste porcelain,
painted in enamel colours
BRISTOL; c.1775
Height 7½ ins.

The earlier Plymouth figures were
usually made to stand on bases
modelled with rococo scrollwork,
but, by 1770, this fashion was
becoming outdated and being
replaced by the more current neo-
Classical styles. A form of base
favoured at the Bristol factory
(1770–81) consisted of a rock-like
mound, somewhat similar to that
used during the Chelsea-Derby
period, but decidedly lower and
less craggy.

Even at this later period
Richard Champion was still
experiencing difficulties with his
firing, and quite a few of his
figures are beginning to heel over
and appear to be in danger of
falling.

Private Collection

Plate 51

Cream-jug; hard-paste porcelain, with underglaze-blue, transfer-printed decoration STAFFORDSHIRE (New Hall China Manufactory); *c*.1782–87 Height $3\frac{3}{4}$ ins.

In 1781 a group of six Staffordshire potters, John Turner, Anthony Keeling, Samuel Hollins, Jacob Warburton, Peter Warburton and John Daniel, purchased 'the whole art, mystery and patent' concerned with the manufacture of hard-paste porcelain, from Richard Champion of the Bristol factory. Together they then set up the New Hall China Manufactory which continued in production until 1835.

With the abolition of the English tea-tax in 1784, there was a greater demand for cheap, but refined tea-wares which would compete in every way with the mass of imported Chinese porcelain. These wares included teapots, often with matching stands, sugar-pots, tea-bowls (without handles), teacups and saucers, slop-bowls, plates and jugs. All these wares were produced by New Hall in their hard-paste porcelain together with similarly decorated pieces for the making and drinking of coffee.

Apart from the well-known polychrome enamel sprig patterns, many New Hall wares were decorated with underglaze-blue transfer-prints. These prints were of a richer colour than those found on the earlier hard-paste Plymouth and Bristol wares, probably due to

Formerly Gilbert Bradley Collection

the lower firing temperature and softer glaze used at this later factory. Their patterns, as illustrated, were mostly based on those painted on the Chinese export porcelain of the same period. This jug also illustrates what is now accepted as a very characteristic New Hall handle, where the thumb-rest is formed by overlapping the two sections of the handle (sometimes referred to by today's collectors as the 'clip handle').

Plate 52

Cup and saucer; bone-china,
painted in enamel colours
Mark: N185 (pattern number)
STAFFORDSHIRE (New Hall);
c.1820
Diameter (of saucer) $5\frac{1}{4}$ ins.

Faced with competition from the many other Staffordshire potters who, from the early years of the 19th century, were producing the more popular bone-china, the New Hall potters also decided to abandon the manufacture of hard-paste in favour of the new material. The various pattern numbers used on the two bodies suggest that the changeover took place in about 1814. Bone-china patterns are usually those numbering from about 1,000, but certain of the earlier numbered patterns, which were introduced during the 'hard-paste' period, can also be found on the later wares.

The only marks frequently used on the hard-paste New Hall porcelain were the pattern numbers, either alone or with 'N' or 'No', painted in various enamel colours, but usually crimson or black. A few of the blue-and-white wares, as discussed, were sometimes marked with an underglaze-blue version of a crowned rampant lion, as used on the German porcelain of Frankenthal. A printed mark of 'New Hall' within a double lined circle is a mark quite often seen on their bone-china, especially saucers.

Plate 53

Plate; soft-paste porcelain, painted
in enamel colours and gilt, by a
London decorator
Mark: 'NANTGARW/C.W'
impressed
WELSH (Nantgarw, Billingsley's
factory); *c*.1817
Diameter 9½ ins.

William Billingsley, the painter credited with the painting of so many
roses, led a very chequered career before eventually starting his own
porcelain factory at Nantgarw in South Wales. He was born in Derby in
1758 and apprenticed as a porcelain painter to William Duesbury at the
Derby factory in 1774. Remaining there until 1796, he gained a very
high reputation as a flower-painter in a naturalistic style. Billingsley then
produced his own porcelain at Pinxton until 1799, after which he was
engaged in enamelling various other potters' wares at Mansfield and
Torksey, before spending five years helping to perfect a porcelain body
for the Worcester factory.

In 1813 Billingsley set up his own porcelain factory at Nantgarw,
aided by his two daughters Lavinia and Sarah and his son-in-law Samuel
Walker. He was financed by a Mr. Wm. Weston Young, who became a
partner in the firm. Due to shortage of funds Billingsley endeavoured,
unsuccessfully, to get a government subsidy to continue his venture. His

request was drawn to the attention of Mr. Dillwyn, the proprietor of the Cambrian earthenware pottery at Swansea, who persuaded Billingsley to move his manufacture to Swansea. Billingsley remained at Swansea from 1814 until 1817, when he returned to Nantgarw until about 1820. It is reputed Billingsley took up employment with John Rose, at the Coalport factory, where he remained until his death in 1828.

The fine quality soft-paste porcelain produced by Billingsley during both his Nantgarw periods was in great demand by London dealers, including Mortlocks of Oxford Street, who purchased the wares in the white glazed state, and then had them decorated to order by London enamellers in what is now considered to be too ornate a style.

Plate 54

Plate; soft-paste porcelain, decorated with enamel colours and gilt
Mark: 'SWANSEA' (in red)
WELSH (Swansea, Dillwyn's factory); *c*.1815
Diameter 8¼ ins.

Private Collection

In order to produce a more stable and less costly material, the paste made after Billingsley's arrival at Swansea was modified with the addition of other ingredients, which resulted in a so-called 'duck-egg' green translucency. Many of the table-wares made from this paste were decorated by notable flower-painters trained by Billingsley. This plate was probably painted by David Evans, who excelled at painting wild-flowers and garden-flowers, including roses, in a crisp, bold manner with strong colours.

After Billingsley returned to Nantgarw, Dillwyn leased the Swansea porcelain works to T. & J. Bevington, who produced a very inferior porcelain, sometimes marked with impressed crossed tridents.

Victoria and Albert Museum

Plate 55

Dish; porcelain, decorated with a
'bat-printed' landscape
Mark: 'SPODE' painted in red
enamel and number 557
STAFFORDSHIRE (Spode's
factory); *c*.1810
Length 11 ins.

The normal method of transferring printed designs from engraved
copperplates onto ceramic wares was with fine tissue paper but, in the
early-19th century, a method referred to as 'bat-printing', a technique
frequently used by the firms of Spode, Minton, Mason, and a few others,
became very popular.

The process used a copperplate into which the required pattern was
stipple-engraved (that is, was composed of minute dots, instead of
engraved lines). Oil, instead of cobalt or an enamel colour, was then
rubbed into the engraving. Next a 'bat' or thin sheet of gelatinous glue
was used to transfer the oiled pattern from the copperplate onto the
glazed surface of the ware to be decorated. The enamel colour was then
dusted onto the oiled impression with a lock of carded cotton. This
process resulted in a much softer reproduction than the use of line-
engraved plates, and the landscapes, which were so often used, took on a
'misty morning' effect, as illustrated.

60

Plate 56

Pair of spill vases; bone-china,
painted in enamel colours and gilt
Mark: 'SPODE' painted in black
STAFFORDSHIRE (Spode's
factory); c.1810–20
Height 4⅛ ins.

John Warrell Collection

These two spill vases are surely the most charming of this class of ware ever produced, the inscriptions combining with the flower painting to read 'Walk upon [roses] and [forget-me-not]'.

From about 1805 Josiah Spode II had come to a rather unusual arrangement with the firm of Messrs. Daniel and Brown, as they appear to have actually worked within the factory of Spode, more in the capacity of sub-contractors, carrying out the enamelling and gilding of many of the wares produced at the factory. This would, of course, have excluded the large range of earthenwares decorated with underglaze-blue transfer-prints. This same firm of Daniel and Brown also had premises at Hanley where they decorated wares for other manufacturers.

The partnership of Daniel and Brown was dissolved early in 1806, but Henry Daniel and his workers continued to work with Spode until about 1820, when Henry Daniel and his son Richard established their own pottery and porcelain manufactories at Stoke and Shelton. Henry Daniel died in 1841, but the son continued to run the Stoke concern.

In his book, *Spode*, Leonard Whiter has compiled an interesting list of pattern numbers used by Spode, together with the years, approximately, when the patterns were introduced. The life of a pattern depended upon its popularity, but the numbers introduced during the Daniel association appear to range from about 1,056 to around 3,750.

Plate 57

Dessert dish; porcelain, painted in
underglaze-blue
Probably Staffordshire (Mason's
factory); early-19th century
Length 8¼ ins.

Miles Mason (*b*.1752) was first concerned with the importation of
Chinese porcelain in about 1780; a business he came into through
marriage. He was prompted to become a ceramic manufacturer himself,
and took a partnership in a Liverpool pottery under the management of
Thomas Wolfe and John Davenport. (The company later changed to
Thomas Wolfe & Co.) This partnership, and another between Mason and
George Wolfe of Lane Delph, Staffordshire, were dissolved in 1800.

There seems little doubt that during his early years as a pottery
manufacturer Mason was concerned solely in the production of
porcelain, first at the Victoria Pottery in Lane Delph, and then at what
later became the Minerva Works in Fenton, Staffordshire, from about
1807. He was joined here by his son George, who in later years was
joined by his brother Charles. The brothers continued to run the Lane
Delph works after the death of their father in 1822, but they were by
then only concerned with the manufacture of their Patent Ironstone
China.

Both the upper edge and base of the foot-rim of this dish have been
deliberately coloured to an orange-brown, a feature usually only present
on Chinese export wares. This suggests that the piece might well have
been made as a replacer for an Oriental dish. In an advertisement of 1804
it was stated that Mason 'proposes to renew or match the impaired or
broken services of the nobility and gentry . . .'

Plate 58

Cup and saucer; bone-china,
painted in enamel colours
STAFFORDSHIRE (Minton's
Factory); *c.*1820
Diameter (saucer) 5½ ins.

Thomas Minton (*b.*1765) started his career as an apprentice to Thomas
Turner at Caughley. It was there he learnt the art of engraving the
copperplates used for transfer-printing designs onto porcelain or
earthenware. Minton then worked for several other major Staffordshire
potters before establishing his own factory, at Stoke, in 1793.

Up until recently it had not been possible to say definitely whether
certain table-wares, ornamental vases, etc., and a particular class of figures
were of the Minton factory. Some of the original early-19th century
pattern books were then made available by the present-day Minton
concern. The fine hand-painted illustrations in these books have enabled
collectors and museums to identify many of their pieces with certainty,
despite the fact that they bear no factory-marks.

The pleasing pattern seen here, with the typical Minton 'ring' handle
appears to be original to the factory, but it is interesting to note that they
also produced many wares after the designs of such factories as Nantgarw
and Worcester. From 1842 Minton also used a year symbol, a different
device or letter being impressed into the clay for each year up until 1942.

Victoria and Albert Museum

Plate 59

Dish of walnuts; bone-china,
painted in natural colours
STAFFORDSHIRE (Minton's
factory); *c*.1825–30
Diameter 6½ ins.

This very realistically coloured dish of walnuts is typical of the type of
unmarked wares that have in the past been attributed to such factories as
Coalport, prior to the Minton factory pattern books being made
available. Various sizes of this same perforated plate were used at Mintons
to contain equally well modelled and painted garden peas or fruit and
flowers.

The early Minton pattern book now available covers the period from
about 1825 to about 1840, when a second dated book continues to list
their ornamental wares with pattern number 256. The perforated plate
shown here with the walnuts is illustrated in the earlier book as No. 73.

64

Plate 60

Cup and saucer; bone-china,
painted in enamel colours and gilt
Mark: 'WEDGWOOD' printed
in red
STAFFORDSHIRE (Wedgwood's
factory); 1812–22
Diameter (of saucer) $5\frac{5}{8}$ ins.

Josiah Wedgwood, who died in 1795, considered all forms of porcelain as being very inferior to the fine earthenware and stoneware he perfected for his productions of classical-styled wares.

The new material of bone-china, said to have been introduced by Josiah Spode in 1794, became very popular and was soon adopted by numerous other major potteries. It was in 1812 that Josiah Wedgwood II introduced bone-china to Wedgwood's range of wares, probably in order to increase their sales and help to remedy the huge losses they suffered in export trade during the Napoleonic Wars. This material was produced by Wedgwoods until 1822, during which time some cups and saucers were very tastefully decorated with landscapes by John Cutts, or flowers in the contemporary fashion. The mark used for these wares consisted of the word 'WEDGWOOD' printed in red, blue or gilt. This material was not used again until about 1878, when a small printed version of the Portland Vase was used as a mark. This mark was a rather unsuitable choice, since the Wedgwood reproductions, made in 1790, of this famous vase, were of jasperware, a close-grained stoneware.

Plate 61

Vase; bone-china, decorated with
enamel colours and gilt
Mark: a griffin printed in puce and
'Rockingham Works, Brameld,
Manufacturers to the King'
ROCKINGHAM; *c*.1835
Height 14¾ ins.

Pottery had been produced at the
factory of Swinton, in South
Yorkshire, since about the middle
of the 18th century. It was in 1806
that the works were taken over by
John Brameld and his son William,
and later three younger sons,
Thomas, John Wager and George
Frederick. But it was not until
1826 that the Bramelds started to
manufacture a very fine quality
china of a clear white translucent
body, covered with a glaze that
often shows signs of minute
crazing. As a result of financial
difficulties, probably brought
about by the rather extravagant
styles of decoration used,
production was forced to
terminate in 1842.

The so-called 'Rockingham'
style was very similar to those of
several other contemporary
factories, many of whom were
also producing wares of a
'neo-rococo' style. This was not
really a revival of the
18th-century rococo style, but
was more a blend between
classical and rococo, as is well
illustrated on this fine vase.
During their 'porcelain years'
Rockingham productions
consisted primarily, however, of
well decorated dessert, tea and
coffee services, usually featuring
attractive ground colours of

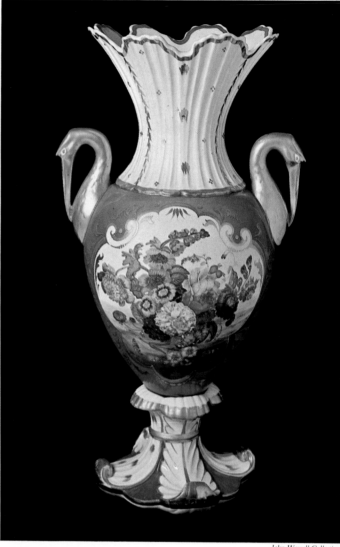

John Warrell Collection

various tones of blue, green, red, grey or buff. They are known to have
included about four hundred different dessert services and around one
thousand various patterned tea and coffee services.

The Bramelds were aided financially by the Earl Fitzwilliam, on
whose estate the pottery was built. A *griffin passant*, the family crest of the
Fitzwilliams was used as their trade-mark. When printed in red the mark
dates from 1826–30, after which it was printed in puce. The term
'Rockingham' was adopted to commemorate the late Marquis, from
whom the Earl inherited the property.

Plate 62

Ewer; hard-paste porcelain,
lustrous glaze
Mark: Tower, wolfhound and
harp (printed)
IRISH (Belleek); *c*.1870
Height 9½ ins.

As more collectors of ceramics
seek out the ever fewer available
objects, wares which, up until a
few years ago, were easily
obtainable are now more difficult
to find. Among this class are the
porcelains made at the town of
Belleek in County Fermanagh.

The actual date when the
factory was first established is a
little vague, but wares were
apparently being produced in
commercial quantities by 1863. It
was R. W. Armstrong who was
initially responsible for the
production of the hard-paste
Parian-type of body, made more
attractive than the Parian wares of
mid-19th century Staffordshire, by
the addition of a glaze which when
fired took on a mother-of-pearl
iridescence. The firm traded under
the name of the partner,
D. McBirney. Apart from flower-
encrusted articles as shown, many
vases, dishes and centrepieces were
produced in the form of shells,
together with sea-weed and other
marine subjects.

The collector seeking the earlier
wares of this factory should avoid
those with the harp and Irish
wolfhound mark which include
the word 'Ireland'. This word was
not added to the mark until after
1891, following the American
McKinley Tariff Act.

Private Collection

MARKS

CHELSEA, incised triangle mark of
c.1745–49.

CHELSEA, applied anchor mark,
c.1749–52.

CHELSEA, red enamel anchor,
c.1752–58.

CHELSEA, gold anchor, c.1758–70,
and often later.

CHELSEA, 'crown and trident' in
underglaze-blue, c.1748–50.

CHELSEA-DERBY, variety of marks
used between 1770–84, usually in gold.

BOW, incised and impressed 'repairers'
marks used from c.1750–60.

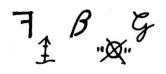

BOW, selection of painters' marks used
between 1750–70, in underglaze-blue.

BOW, 'anchor and dagger' mark in
red enamel, c.1762–76.

DERBY, painted in blue, purple or
black from about 1782–1800, in red
from c.1800–25.

DERBY, incised mark used on 'biscuit'
figures from about 1782–1800.

DERBY, mark printed in red enamel
during Bloor period, c.1825–40.

DERBY, printed in red enamel,
c.1830–48.

PINXTON, red, and purple enamel
marks, 1796–1813.

WORCESTER, 'Crescent' mark, used
from about 1755–90, the later 'filled-
in' form of crescent usually used with
printed decoration in underglaze-blue.
The underglaze-blue 'W' used from
c.1755–70.

WORCESTER, the 'fretted square'
mark, in underglaze-blue from
c.1755–75. This mark is often seen on
hard-paste porcelain reproductions.

WORCESTER, numbers 1–9 written
as Chinese characters in underglaze-
blue, c.1775–85.

WORCESTER, Flight period, various
painted forms of the name used from
1783–92. Crown added in 1788.

Flight & Barr

WORCESTER, Flight & Barr period,
various painted forms of the partnership used between 1793–1807.

BFB

WORCESTER, Barr, Flight & Barr
period, impressed mark of c.1807–13.

FBB

WORCESTER, Flight, Barr & Barr
period, impressed mark of about
1813–20.

WORCESTER, Chamberlain's factory, early written mark of c.1786–
1810.

GRAINGER LEE & CO
WORCESTER

WORCESTER, Grainger, Lee & Co's
factory, c.1812–39, early written mark.

Salopian Sx

CAUGHLEY, c.1772–1799, common
form of impressed mark. Printed mark
'S' for Salopian in underglaze-blue,
c.1775–90.

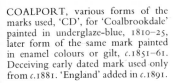

COALPORT, various forms of the
marks used, 'CD', for 'Coalbrookdale'
painted in underglaze-blue, 1810–25,
later form of the same mark painted
in enamel colours or gilt, c.1851–61.
Deceiving early dated mark used only
from c.1881. 'England' added in c.1891.

PLYMOUTH, hard-paste porcelain,
sign for tin, painted in underglaze-blue,
blue enamel, red or gold from 1768–70.

BRISTOL, hard-paste porcelain,
painted marks used from 1770–81.

NEW HALL, painted enamel pattern
number, usually in red, crimson or
black, 1781–c.1835.

NEW HALL, printed mark used on
bone-china from c.1812–35.

MINTON, form of painted mark
used from c.1800–30, often on wares
decorated in Sèvres fashion.

MINTON, selection of year cyphers
used from 1842. These impressed marks
indicate 1884, 1858 and 1879.

SWANSEA

NANT GARW
C.W

SWANSEA & NANTGARW, im-
pressed mark of 'SWANSEA' used
between 1814–22. The Nantgarw
mark impressed with 'C.W' for 'China
Works' used between c.1813–14 and
1817–c.22. Painted versions of these
marks have been added to later wares
of other factories.

ROCKINGHAM, the 'griffin' mark
printed in red enamel from c.1826–30,
and then in puce up to about 1842.
Reddish-brown versions of this mark is
sometimes seen on hard-paste porcelain
reproductions.

WEDGWOOD

WEDGWOOD, mark printed on
bone-china from c.1812–22, in red or
blue enamel, or gilt.

MASON, MILES, printed mark on
porcelain from c.1800–1816.

BELLEEK, printed or impressed mark
used from 1863–91, after which
'Co.FERMANAGH, IRELAND' was
added.

This mark indicates that the design or
form of the piece has been registered
with the Patent Office sometime
between 1842 and 1883, the exact date
can be arrived at by consulting the
recommended mark-books (See Bibliography). This example dates to 6th
January (C), 1868 (X), the '12' is the
reference to the 'parcel' of patterns
registered on the same day. From
January 1884, this device was abandoned and the simple 'Rd' or 'Rd.No.'
was used, totalling over 550,000 by
1909.

Fuller details of these marks and others
may be obtained from the books
referred to in the Bibliography, all by
the same author.

GLOSSARY

BISCUIT	a once-fired ceramic body, without glaze
BOCAGE	a screen of ceramic leaves and flowers to form a background to a figure or group
BODY	an alternative name used to describe a type of ceramic ware, e.g. stoneware body, hard-paste body, etc.
camaïeu	decoration painted in various tones of one colour (monochrome)
CHINA-CLAY	a white refractory clay formed over a long period from decomposed granite
CHINA-STONE	a fusible stone which when fired at about 1350°C, together with china-clay, forms a hard, white, translucent material of hard-paste porcelain.
CRAZING	a fault in the glaze resulting in minute surface cracks, only rarely seen on hard-paste porcelain
Deutsche Blumen	naturalistic flower-painting as introduced at Meissen in about 1740
ENAMEL	a form of coloured glass used for decoration of ceramics by fusing to the glaze at a temperature of about 800°C.
famille rose	a style of Chinese porcelain decoration used from the early 18th century, and including pinks and crimsons derived from chloride of gold
FRIT	a form of the ingredients of glass, used in soft-paste porcelain as an alternative to china-stone
GLOST-KILN	a kiln used to fuse the glaze to a ceramic ware
HARD-PASTE PORCELAIN	the type of porcelain first introduced by the Chinese potter, made from china-clay and china-stone
KAOLIN	the Chinese term for china-clay, meaning 'high-ridge'
LUSTRE DECORATION	metallic colours fused to the surface of wares in a reduction kiln, copper resulting in copper-coloured tones, silver firing to a brassy yellow, chloride of gold looking like copper when applied to a red-brown clay body, and appearing as pink on a white surface. Platinum was used to give the effect of silver

LUTING	the fixing of relief decoration or the assembling of parts of figures or wares by the use of watered-down clay (slip)
MOULDING	the shaping of clay with the use of prepared moulds. The clay is used in a plastic state and hand-pressed into the hollow moulds
MUFFLE-KILN	the low-firing kiln (about 800°C) used for applying enamel colours to ceramics
PARIAN WARE	a white ceramic body introduced about 1840, used primarily for the scaled-down reproduction of full-size sculpture. Also used to a certain extent for decorative and table-wares
PETUNTSE	the Chinese term for the prepared china-stone, meaning 'little white bricks'
REPAIRER	the name of the tradesman who assembles the various moulded, or cast sections of a ceramic figure, or vessel, with the aid of slip
REDUCTION KILN	a kiln in which a smoky atmosphere is deliberately obtained
SLIP-CASTING	the forming of clay wares or figures by pouring slip into hollow plaster-of-Paris moulds, the plaster absorbs the water from the slip and in doing so builds up a thin layer of clay on the inside wall of the mould, the surplus slip is then emptied away, and after a short period the cast can be removed from the mould
SLIP	watered-down clay of any ceramic body, to a thin creamy consistency
SOFT-PASTE PORCELAIN	artificial porcelain made from various white-firing clays and the ingredients of glass, bone-ash, or steatite, etc.
SPRIGGING	the applying of separately moulded decoration to the surface of wares
THROWING	the age-old process of forming a hollow circular form from clay by hand, with the use of a rotating turntable
TRANSFER-PRINTING	the transferring of a design engraved into a copperplate, or wood-block, by means of a thin paper or slab of gelatine, to the surface of the body or glaze of a ceramic ware. High temperature colours are applied prior to glazing, low-temperature enamels are fused onto the glaze
WASTERS	faulty wares, usually sought as evidence of manufacture on the sites of old potteries

BIBLIOGRAPHY

WATNEY, B. *Longton Hall Porcelain* (Faber & Faber 1957)

LANE, A. E. *English Porcelain Figures of the 18th Century* (Faber & Faber 1961)

RICE, D. G. *Rockingham Ornamental Porcelain* (Ceramic Book Co. 1966)

GODDEN, G. A. *Minton Porcelain of the First Period* (Herbert Jenkins 1968)

GODDEN, G. A. *Coalport and Coalbrookdale Porcelains* (Herbert Jenkins 1970)

WHITER, L. *Spode* (Barrie & Jenkins 1970)

BARRETT, F. A. AND THORPE, A. L. *Derby Porcelain* (Faber & Faber 1971)

HOLGATE, D. F. *New Hall and Its Imitators* (Faber & Faber 1971)

LOCKETT, T. A. *Davenport Pottery and Porcelain* (David & Charles 1972)

SHREWSBURY ART GALLERY *Caughley Porcelain. Bi-Centenary Exhibition* (Shrewsbury Art Gallery 1972)

BEMROSE, PAUL *The Pomona Potworks, Newcastle, Staffs* (Transactions of the English Ceramic Circle. Vol. 9 Pts. 1 and 3. 1973 and 1975)

EAGLESTONE, A. A. AND LOCKETT, T. A. *The Rockingham Pottery* (David & Charles 1973)

WATNEY, B. *English Blue and White Porcelain of the 18th Century* (Faber & Faber 1973)

SANDON, H. *Worcester Porcelain 1751–1793* (Barrie & Jenkins 1974)

SAVAGE, G. AND NEWMAN, H. *Illustrated Dictionary of Ceramics* (Thames & Hudson 1974)

SMITH, SHEENAH *Lowestoft Porcelain in Norwich Castle Museum* (Norfolk Museum Services 1975)

CUSHION, J. P. *Pocket-Book of British Ceramic Marks* (Faber & Faber (New Ed.) 1976)

AUSTIN, J. C. *Chelsea Porcelain at Colonial Williamburg* (Colonial Williamburg Foundation 1977)

CUSHION, J. P. *Pottery and Porcelain Tablewares* (Studio Vista 1977)

HONEY, W. B. *Old English Porcelain* (Faber & Faber 1977)

HAGGAR, R. G. AND ADAMS, ELIZABETH *Mason Porcelain and Ironstone 1796–1853* (Faber & Faber 1977)

BRADLEY, H. F. G. (Ed.) *Ceramics of Derbyshire* (Bradley 1978)

SANDON, H. *Flight and Barr Worcester Porcelain 1783–1840* (The Antique Collectors Club 1978)

CUSHION, J. P. *Handbook of Pottery and Porcelain Marks* (Faber & Faber (New Ed.) 1980)

TWITCHETT, J. *Derby Porcelain* (Barrie & Jenkins 1980)

ADAMS, ELIZABETH AND REDSTONE, D. *Bow Porcelain and the Bow Factory* (Faber & Faber 1981)

BRANYON, L., FRENCH, H. AND SANDON, J. *Worcester Blue and White Porcelain 1751–1790* (Barrie & Jenkins 1981)

GODDEN, G. A. *Caughley and Worcester Porcelain 1775–1800* (Antique Collectors Club 1981)

	DATE DUE		